POETRY

THAT

HEALS

POETRY THAT HEALS

Naomi Beth Wakan

Shanti Arts Publishing

Brunswick, Maine

POETRY THAT HEALS

Published by Shanti Arts Publishing
Cover and interior design by Shanti Arts Designs

Shanti Arts LLC
Brunswick, Maine
www.shantiarts.com

Printed in the United States of America

Previously published in 2014 by
Pacific-Rim Publishers,
Victoria, British Columbia, Canada

All unattributed poetry is by Naomi Beth Wakan. All
photographs in the text are ©Elias Wakan (www.elias-
wakan.com), except for those in the chapter on haiga,
which are by Carol MacRury and Jim Swift.
Cover image is by Christine Cote.

ISBN: 978-1-947067-28-8 (softcover)
ISBN: 978-1-947067-29-5 (digital)

LCCN: 2017964362

DEFINITIONS

choka
classical Japanese long poem

ginko
a haiku-producing walk

haibun
autobiographical prose with haiku

haiga
haiku with artwork

haijin
writer of haiku

haikai
term for haiku and its related genres

haiku (in English)
three-line poem using sensory images

renku
linked poetry

senryu
humorous haiku

tanka (in English)
five-line poem

waka
name for tanka in the Japanese classical period

CONTENTS

PREFACE

In this inspired memoir, Naomi Beth Wakan's exuberance is palpable on every page as she leads us on a journey through the realms of haikai; that is, haiku and its related genres. Along the way we encounter many of the often controversial "rules" that attend the various forms. Naomi has considered the importance of these tenets without becoming ensnared. With resolve, and what Buddhism terms "the way-seeking mind," she has reached the heart of what these forms, particularly haiku, have to offer: a deep and abiding appreciation for this ephemeral moment, an appreciation that transcends the written word. For Naomi, the journey has been both joyous and cathartic. By sharing her insights, she encourages us to discover for ourselves the gifts of haikai.

— Christopher Herold, founding editor of *The Heron's Nest*

The Uses for Poetry

Who has not
at times of distress
sighed, groaned, cried
and let out an anguished
"Why?"
And at such times,
who has not written
"Why?" down a hundred times
and followed with
a plea of some kind
to make the trouble go away?
And, as the distress
takes form on paper,
who has not added
an urgent call for help?
In this way poems are made.
And
when the first robin returns
and the first green shoots
pierce through the earth,
who has not,
at such times,
sung out with optimism
that all will be well
with the earth someday,
and that lovers will find each other
and that neighborhoods will flourish?
At such times,
who doesn't jot down a line
to record pleasure
at cool, clear mornings,

and radiant sunsets?
And perhaps a word, or two
is added to the page
that this day might possibly
turn out better than others?
And so, we find,
that in our joy
a poem has been born.

Yes,
at such bitter and such sweet times
poetry has its uses, I find.

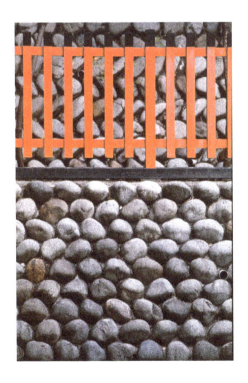

INTRODUCTION

This is the story of a poetry journey. My poetry journey. It began somewhere in my middle years with a stay of two years in Japan. The first thing I wanted to do there was to translate a Japanese friend's book of haiku into English; at the time I knew hardly more than a few words of Japanese and had just met up with haiku for the first time in my life. That kind of limitation has never stopped me. I called in another Japanese friend, who taught English to children, and she did the first awkward translation into English. Then I speedily whipped the words back into poetic form. From that period on, I was hooked on haiku.

That hooking lasted nearly thirty years. It included me meeting Winona Baker, a brilliant haijin (haiku writer), whose lovely book *Moss-hung Trees* had such a big influence on me. Soon I became a member of Haiku Canada, and as volunteers were scarce, I found myself volunteered — and accepted rather unwillingly — to be the Western Canada regional coordinator. I had no idea what my duties were to be, so I invented the idea that the regional coordinator should coordinate a gathering of haijin from the regions of British Columbia and the Yukon.

I chose my birthday for what became an annual gathering. This decision resulted from an incident I recall from my childhood when my twin and I were standing in the kitchen of my grandmother's boarding house, and a strange young man was giving us presents. He said it was his birthday. I remember that we giggled at the idea that he should give presents on his birthday, because we knew that birthdays were days when one got presents, not gave them.

As I started to think of gathering the haijin from the region together, I thought of this incident and decided it would be my birthday gift to everyone that I would organize and host such a meeting. The annual summer meeting grew from one day to two and a half days and from one occasion to twelve years. During those years I met some of the best haiku and tanka writers in North America: Michael Dylan Welch, Christopher Herold, Jim Kacian, Terry Ann Carter, Carole MacRury, Susan Constable, Vicki McCullough, Alice Frampton, and Amelia Fielden (from Australia), to name but a few.

They assumed I was a haijin, so I didn't bother disillusioning them. However, it was from these masters that I really learned how to write haiku. I felt differently about the process than I did at the time I began. I was a beginner again, but not a beginner.

first there were haiku
then there were no haiku
then there were haiku

Sometime after I became absorbed in writing haiku, Sonja Arntzen attended one of my writing workshops. She was an academic, recently retired, wondering how to change her academic writing style to one that a more general readership could handle. Sonja just happens to be a scholar of classical Japanese literature and, luckily for me, lives on my little island of Gabriola. She became my guide into tanka, that five-line predecessor of haiku.

As the haiku weekends developed, we introduced tanka and also haibun (haiku embedded in prose), haiga (haiku plus artwork), and finally renku (group poetry writing). As I learned more about each of these poetry forms, my horizons seemed to shoot open. Somehow the more Japanese poetry styles I met up with, the faster my creative energies flowed. I wrote hundreds of haiku and tanka and, with others, tried at least half a dozen jointly written renku.

Each Saturday afternoon of those annual meetings was reserved for a ginko (a haiku-producing walk) and afterwards a critiquing of our efforts. It was these couple of hours every year that taught me more about haiku than I could have ever learned from books.

So, in *Poetry that Heals* I will speak of the power of both writing and reading haiku, the opening to oneself that tanka offers, and the opening to others that response tanka allows. I'll end with the teamwork of renku that demands trust and took me into community.

Many of the classical haiku masters were also lay monks, and although I have no spiritual label, you will find touches of Buddha's Four Noble Truths throughout the book. These are that (1) all is dukkha — suffering, anxiety, unsatisfactoriness; (2) there is a cause for dukkha — our constant craving for happiness; (3) there can be a cessation of dukkha; and (4) there is a path leading to the cessation of dukkha, the path being the Eightfold Path of Right View, Right Intention, Right Speech, Right Action, Right Livelihood, Right Effort, Right Mindfulness, and Right Concentration.

You will find no mention of "life force," "spiritual," "inner voice," "sacred space," or other such terms in this recounting of my journey. These words are just not part of my vocabulary. I like to be as clear and exact as possible, and that requires not using concepts I would have trouble defining.

I am not a poet of excesses; my choice is usually the middle way, my favorite position is on the fence of "maybes." I am not aiming at perfection for myself, nor enlightenment or any other of those extremes that are far too nebulous and exhausting. Idealism has a high failure rate. I am about empowerment, not defeat.

Looking back on the last nearly thirty years of writing poetry, I have never considered it a journey that I was consciously taking. I never once thought: *I am getting healthy* or *I am growing wiser*. It is only on reflection that I can see the growth that has happened to me in my pursuit of poetry.

By taking you along on my journey, perhaps you, too, by stopping a moment at signposts, by pausing to consider a view, might find clues for your own poetry path.

the signpost
knocked over by the wind . . .
our road points to heaven

BEING HERE NOW

So what is haiku, that poetry form that started me out on a nearly thirty-year journey during which poetry became my pathway and also my guide?

> *Poetry has an interesting function.*
> *It helps people "be" where they are.*
>
> — Gary Snyder

Haiku (the same word is used for both singular and plural), as written in English, are three-line poems that focus on the seasons and how they are recorded by our senses. They usually contain two images juxtaposed in a way that not only defines the moment, but does so in such a penetrating way that each image is augmented by the other. What Snyder says about poetry in general can be more properly assigned to describing haiku, for haiku describe the moment and so help someone, for a brief flash, to be on a particular spot at a particular time.

Being in the moment of haiku means that one is not clinging to the past or anxious about the future; everything is in flow, even as we try to still one moment by capturing it in words. When we go with the flow, the sadness that the moment will pass is modified by the joy of spontaneity that being in the moment produces.

Yes, "being where you are" is the essence of haiku. Haiku do not mention your reactions to what you are sensing — as important as they may be — it just records the bare facts, meditation's "bare awareness." The feelings and ideas may be hovering around, but the recording of clear images, sounds, textures, smells, and tastes, using seasonal awareness and supplying two strong images juxtaposed, are all that is required for a good haiku. It's those two strong images that matter. It is those naked images — when caught on the page — that contain, hidden within, all the ideas and feelings that the writer had at the time of writing. The images, in a way, personify William Carlos Williams' statement: "No ideas but in things." The more specifically the image is portrayed, the more the reader will be filled with the feelings, thoughts, and ideas that are only implied in the haiku.

Writing haiku merely asked me to be more aware, more alert to everyday moments, and to use my senses as clearly as possible. Haiku aren't saying anything in the sense of judgment or opinion. Things should not be compared as more or less favorable in haiku. Writing haiku taught me not to cling to cherry blossoms and avoid manure. I began to see that things are neither pleasant nor unpleasant, they just are. I discovered that haiku, because they tell only the bare facts, allowed the objects I was describing to speak for themselves without having my moral judgment, emotional reaction, or intellectual thought put on them. This practice began to be transferred to my day-to-day life when I found myself not rushing to judgment at every turn of events.

Writing haiku, because of the attention I had to pay to the object I was writing about, enabled me to become more impartial, more open, more patient, and because I found I was examining the object I was writing about more carefully, I was not only more interested in outside things, but also less fearful of the things I was describing that I might have considered "unpleasant" before. Keen interest can often overcome phobias.

Abstract terms such as "love", "hate", and "envy" are absent from haiku. Not having to use them allowed me to drop my intellect and emotions and concentrate on my body and using my sense organs in a decisive way.

Whether I was reading or writing haiku, it was their clear images that stilled my chattering mind and fluctuating emotions. Somehow, writing haiku, which limited the words I could actually use to describe what I was sensing (no metaphors, similes, use of few adjectives), opened me to wider horizons where I and the object I was sensing became one; the observer fusing with the observed. When I wrote a haiku, I was not just telling about a piece of sense information, I was describing a piece of information that had grabbed me deeply. The deeper it grabbed me, the deeper my feelings would shine through my description of the object. I didn't analyze my haiku or worry whether it was a "good" haiku or a "bad" haiku (though other poets are very concerned with analysis of what they have written and feel it is an important action). I just wrote what I was sensing.

As a result of continually doing this practice, life has not become something I am constantly evaluating or questioning, it is more something I am experiencing, although it's also true that the "I" that is experiencing blends with the object and, to a certain extent, disappears during the sensing moment that produces the haiku. If I needed to tell something of the moment, I had to do it through the object, but this is very different from me projecting my often neurotic thoughts and emotions onto the object. It is paradoxical that words, the words of haiku, have taken me away from living entirely in words, as it were, to being able to actually experience life.

Being self-conscious, showing how clever you are, aiming for an effect, can be harmful for writing haiku. When I self-consciously wrote a haiku, I found I became too intellectual or too emotional; it was never just me experiencing something. I needed my eight-year-old naïve self back: the child who needed to know why the Emperor had no clothes on.

I began to realize that both in writing haiku and in life I just have to be myself — true to myself, that is.

As I began to become very exact about what I was sensing at one moment, I found that capturing the specific moment opened me to the whole universe, as in Blake's "A world in a grain of sand." I came to realize that a limited space could still allow me access to the whole cosmos. I no longer yearned for a finer home, a more successful career, or to be somewhere, and someone, else. Where I was positioned was sufficient. Oddly enough, the more I became aware of the reality outside myself, the deeper in touch I became with what I can only call "self," while the "I" of the ego seemed to disappear.

Haiku are like "white moments," when everything clicks together and you are totally engaged, totally absorbed, because in these moments you are paradoxically not involved. I found that by "losing my mind," I was somehow tapping into a larger source.

Haiku speak of the ordinary, the everyday. They do not use academic, technical, or complex words. Everything about haiku is simple, unsophisticated, natural, and unpretentious — everything I wished to be in myself. I found that I had to strip away layers of conditioning before I became anywhere near the ordinary genuine human being that I could feel at home with. Haiku is not "Grand Canyon" poetry, it is "A violet by the river's brim" stuff, and it helped me gauge my right size.

I learned so much from the economy of having to get my moment caught in three lines. It was not just the limited space that was the discipline, but also the fact that each word counted for so much and yet the words were simple everyday ones, neither academic, nor complex. For example take Bashō's famous:

on a bare branch
a crow settles
autumn twilight

For me, just the strong nouns — "branch," "crow," "twilight" — were all I needed to tell of seasons passing and the sadness of it all. Bashō could have spoken directly about the ephemeralness of life, and I would have nodded in agreement. Writing the haiku the way he did produced a sigh instead; a sigh that got me wondering whether there isn't some great sadness beyond individual sadness, a great happiness beyond individual happiness, and maybe a great truth beyond individual truths. That is the way of haiku.

I got used to the lack of punctuation and capitals in haiku written in English. Haiku come from somewhere — the past moment — and will disappear into the next moment — the future — so not using a capital letter for starting them and a period to finish them opens the moment to the continuity of life, while not detracting from the idea that I had possibly caught the present — barely. It really amazed me that just the small act of dropping punctuation could open me up to savoring the moment without clinging to it.

I knew already, in some kind of superficial way, from my contact with Buddhism, that all things are imperfect, impermanent, and incomplete, but studying haiku filled all the cells of my body with a "real" knowledge of those facts. Haiku are solid in their own way, yet definitely tentative, definitely imperfect, impermanent, and incomplete.

As for editing haiku, while some poets feel this is important, I learned to rarely edit haiku or even nudge them around, as I cared not about outcome or my own performance. If a haiku didn't seem to click with me, I just tossed it aside. Somehow I learned to trust the creative flow and knew that many more haiku would come my way if I just stopped demanding and clinging.

By writing haiku, by writing those three lines, mentioning a seasonal word and giving sensory details as a necessary basic, I learned that technique, while important, was not going to help me see clearly. For haiku writing demands clear seeing, the ability to make a fresh connection between the images that are being presented. It is the startling freshness that makes the three lines a haiku.

I really started to understand that creativity is seeing connections, and from those connections arise fresh insights. In haiku, the two parts are linked by the way they are juxtaposed, so it is as if each time I wrote a haiku, it was an act of creativity encapsulated in three lines. Moreover, it was the insights I gained from the connections that changed my angle of viewing what I was writing about, and so, by extension, my viewing of the everyday.

Haiku, as I have mentioned, are neutral in moral judgment, nothing is "good" or "bad," it just is. The only shocking thing about haiku is when the familiar is presented in an unfamiliar way. It is always good for the psyche to creep out of its comfort zone, particularly my rather rigid psyche. The problem for me was how to describe the essentials and still stay fresh. I seemed to want to say the same thing over and over again, and yet each presentation demanded that it be different enough to startle the reader — and myself — into a new space.

Perhaps by showing you how I read haiku, you will understand how three small lines had such an effect — albeit over a long period of practice — on my rather cynical and sad way of viewing the world.

READING HAIKU

Haiku don't tell you what to think or what insights they might offer. Haiku present images for readers to consider and then experience the resonances within themselves that the strong images of the haiku produce. The images and the way they are juxtaposed radiate ideas and feelings for the reader by just being intensely themselves. Often for me, direct expression of feelings causes me to shatter, to fall apart; the haiku images' solidity repairs the shards.

the heron
looks at its image
shallow waters

When I read a haiku, whether aloud or to myself, I've found that it's good to read it at least twice: once to get the overall feel; the second time to let it resonate and see where it takes me. Even after the first reading I often find myself already giving that sigh . . . that sigh that means that the haiku has hit its target: my heart. What produces that sigh can actually be listed, I've found. Haiku may be about the mysteriousness of the universe, but what goes into making a "good" haiku is not mysterious. As I tell below why I appreciate each haiku I have chosen, many elements of a "good" haiku will become clear, and you will understand why haiku in general and these haiku in particular are so special to me. By the end of the examples, you will see how a very small poem can send you spinning into outer space; some indeed have spun my life around.

I should point out straight away that haiku are always written in the present tense since they are trying to describe what happened a moment before the poets jot down their haiku. The present tense is used even if poets are not using the moment just past, but a moment from their past. Well, actually, the moment is always past when we take pen to paper, but we have to tell of it as though it is happening as we write. Past or present, it is the intensity of the moment that counts. I call haiku "what, when and where" poetry, since answers to these three questions define the moment.

Haiku derived from the first three lines of a poetry game called renku, where a group of poets alternated offering first three, then two lines in a linked verse. The most distinguished poet present would be asked to start off the long linked verse and would do so by setting the time and place of the gathering, thus choosing words describing that immediate moment. Often, in the hopes that they would be asked to start the renku, poets would prepare these three lines in advance; eventually they detached themselves and became small poems in their own right: haiku.

I will use some of the haiku of people I met during my "haiku period" as a way of saying thank you to them for their generosity.

• • •

empty cabin
the beached canoe
fills with leaves

— Devar Dahl

What a wonderful North American image we have here. It's really like a sketch. Can it be more than a photograph in a scrapbook? It certainly can, because for me it raises questions. The cabin is empty — *who died or left?* The canoe is beached — *is the journey over then?* The leaves have gathered — *is the year or a person's life coming to an end?* These simple desolate images bring up so many thoughts of endings, as well as a certain nostalgia I seem to have for times that were, or maybe never were. Such "haunted" images are often among my favorite haiku. When I read such haiku, it is almost as though I am recreating the scene the poet saw, so closely do I sink into the images that the poet has asked me to consider.

• • •

wishing fountain
outside the cancer clinic
some heads, some tails

— Alice Frampton

Here Alice merely notices that the coins thrown into the fountain have landed, some heads up and some tails up. No comments, no tears. We do not know whether she has taken someone close to her to the clinic, whether it is she, herself, who is a patient, or whether she is just passing by. Yet we do know that healing is a toss-up of uncertain odds, particularly in the case of cancer, which has touched most families, including my own. As a cancer survivor myself, I know what a gamble life is.

By staying in the ordinary, Alice has produced something quite extraordinary here. This economy of haiku — that such a small, everyday image can produce such a strong response in the reader — reflects my own view that staying small in life can provide all one's needs.

On reading, this haiku — *of the senses* — first aroused feelings in me — *as a cancer survivor* — and then intellectual ideas — *about the causes and treatment of cancer* — and intuitions — *about trusting the body and trusting the treatments offered* — thus covering Jung's four cognitive functions — *intuition, intellect, sensing, and feeling,* and all in three lines.

• • •

overcast morning
ripe blackberries
out of reach

— Alice Frampton

Alice is a miraculous haiku writer. Here again she presents a very simple scene that I have experienced so often. As I reach for the ripest blackberries, they are just a little beyond my reach, because any ripe ones close by have been picked by the people who came ahead of me. What a very unsatisfactory moment. This discontent is accentuated by Alice noticing that the morning is overcast. Such juxtaposition is a common technique in haiku. Life is full of such moments. Alice just noticed this one very acutely. By taking a familiar image, she has pronounced a great truth: there is no end to our desires for the unattainable and thus our dissatisfaction with life. The pause after "morning" allows us to sink into the haiku and opens us to what comes next. Such a pause often happens at the end of the first or second line.

• • •

after the garden party   *the garden*
— Ruth Yarrow

This very famous haiku is a simple statement: the writer notices that after all the guests have departed, the garden remains. Who cares about such simplicity? Well I do, for one. This simple observation disorients me as to what reality really is. Does reality need people to experience it? The argument is an old one. Minimal haiku writers often write their haiku in one line.

• • •

moss-hung trees
a deer moves into
the hunter's silence

—Winona Baker

This is the haiku, by a master haiku writer, that motivated me to explore the form. A truly west coast Canadian scene, and there is barely a movement recorded. The moss hangs silently on the trees, the hunter holds his breath, and only the deer takes a few quiet steps forward. It is not the kind of poem that I would write myself, but it is the image of silence that caught me. This haiku brings up so many questions about hunter and hunted, predator and prey, and silence, the silence of the pause at the end of the first line, as we await a second image.

• • •

family visit
he tries to fix what's wrong
with the answering machine

—Winona Baker

Yes, what is wrong with the answering machine? What is wrong with communications in this family? Perhaps the relationship between mother and son is not totally satisfactory? How one small scene can conjure up a Pandora's box of mess that families hold within them. Reading such a haiku reminds me of the relationships between members of my own family when I was growing up, and even now. There's still time to fix the machine, I tell myself. The pause after "visit," as it ends the first line, allows one the surprise of the following image. Those caesurae are important in haiku. Truth is in the gaps.

. . .

it's happened
my mother doesn't know me
autumn rain

— Winona Baker

In this poem, the sadness of autumn, particularly a rainy day in autumn, is not just in the fact that a life is in its decline — for that is where we all must go — but in the fact that the mother is becoming unaware in a world where awareness is such a gift. Alzheimer's is a concern of mine since my half-sisters and my mother all died with their minds wandering. Here, I am reminded that a simple image can stir up major concerns that need to be attended to and not avoided. One doesn't need a whole essay to persuade oneself towards action; three lines are enough.

It seems to me that haiku often reverberate with aloneness. Even though my life when I entered the haiku world was filled with excitement and with the meeting of new people, it was their solitariness that perhaps drew me to the form, since in all my busyness, that is what I needed most. By the way, the middle line swings one to the second image of "rain," which accentuates the sadness of the mother's condition.

• • •

dried up pond
initials in alder bark
scabbed over

— Alice Frampton

The pond is dry and so is the love once shown by a lover carving initials in a tree trunk. Two simple images juxtaposed in a way that accents both — the pond is no longer a pond, and the evidence of love is no longer clear. The haiku records two images that seem disconnected and yet the poet was able to take a leap with her imagination to pair them together. This pairing is what accounts for the creative element in haiku writing.

• • •

blizzard —
in the kitchen throw
the scent of mom

— Alice Frampton

Stormy weather brings up the need for protection, comfort, and security. What better than a throw that holds the lingering scent of the mother to do the job? Haiku is a good medium for opening up the everyday. Small things, if penetrated deeply enough, open to eternity.

. . .

the street-corner preacher
points the way
with his Bible

— Michael Dylan Welch

This is one of Michael's "urban" haiku; no image of the seasons, or even implication of a season, as in traditional haiku, yet still the haiku is very fine. This haiku uses an allusion to another haiku, which was often a traditional thing to do in haiku writing, that is, a reference to an earlier famous haiku. In this case the haiku resembles Issa's:

the man pulling radish
points the way
with a radish

HOW TO WRITE
A HAIKU

Details confuse me,
so when I see a rose,
although I do not know
its pedigree, I write down "rose."
And when I cut it,
I do not know whether
I should cut it on a slant
or straight, or under water twice,
so I write down "cut."
And when I put it in a vase,
I do not know whether it is raku
or glaze, or, perhaps good plastic,
so I write down "vase."
and when I see two red leaves
on the earth beside the rose bush,
I do not know from which tree
they have fallen,
so I write down "red leaves."

And as I set the vase
and the leaves on the table,
I write down

rose just cut
beside the vase
two red leaves

And although I do not know
the details of what I have just done,
the sadness of it all
cracks my heart open.

GINKO — THE
HAIKU WALK

When we lived in Vancouver, we were nature-starved. We sought out parks and roamed beaches. It is true that living in the city does not deny one an awareness of the ephemeralness of things, for decay can be evidenced everywhere, not just in nature. You do not have to go to exotic places or put yourself in unusual situations in order to write haiku; the everyday is enough. In fact, it is where you should be. However, on Gabriola Island, it can't be denied that the natural world is more evident than in the city.

We moved to Gabriola about the time I got immersed in haiku, as if my body knew it needed this move. Nature became my development path. Although I didn't look much at the stars or learn the names of more than a few plants, it was nature all the way to the village stores, nature up to the mail box, and nature out the back and front doors. I was living in ginko land. It is the linking of the seasons to human nature that makes haiku such a healing thing. If truth comes from observing nature, then haiku writing is the way to search it out. Haiku writing tied me to the seasons' rhythms and also to my own.

Gin means "making a poem," and *ko* means "going." A ginko is a walk, usually in a natural setting, done so one can be stimulated to write haiku. Often it is done at the start of a season such as cherry-blossom time, or at solstices or equinoxes. You can, of course, take a ginko on your own, but usually it is done with a group of people, who sometimes have a leader and sometimes don't. Occasionally, they might be given a theme. Haiku and haiku writing can be discussed during the walk, other topics can occupy the conversation, or it can be done in silence.

Masaoka Shiki, who lived at the end of the nineteenth century and was one of Japan's four major haiku masters, promoted what he called shasei, "sketching from life," and ginko is certainly that.

When we first settled on Gabriola we were down in the nearby beach park every day, and I became intensely attentive for haiku moments. It was as if I was on constant alert; relaxed, but somehow acutely aware. Aware of when the ducks arrived and when the herring run was happening; aware of the old farm meadow that was part of the park; and aware of when the first Camas and Spring Gold appeared. It just seemed that this was what my body wanted to do most. And so that is what it did. I was not just taking the ginko in order to write a splendid haiku, but to increase my awareness.

If you are intent on getting to some goal at any price, you've pretty well blown the pleasure of the whole venture. Aiming to write good haiku is fruitless. Writing haiku is effortless, you can't force them to come to you in any way. You can only prepare by having the necessary techniques at your fingertips.

Of course, I could have gone on ginko in Vancouver, but I was too eaten up with ambitions for Pacific-Rim Publishers, our small educational publishing house that we were establishing at that time, to have time for anything else.

With Pacific-Rim Publishers, I was always concerned with sales, promotion, the best table at book fairs, the most bookings at school Professional Days. I was totally wrapped up in the firm, and everything I did and everybody I met revolved around sales. I didn't have time for anything else. This frenzy of activity made me into a person I didn't recognize.

The clear seeing demanded in the writing of haiku should be absent of ambition, competition, and jealousy. One must be like a small child saying "Wow!" Only it doesn't have to have the unusualness a "Wow!" usually indicates, just the freshness. By writing haiku, I learned not to invest a lot of my time aiming for perfection, winning prizes, getting noticed, making sales; it would all come to nought. I began to learn to relax and really live my life.

The more I wrote haiku, the more I stopped worrying about results and started enjoying the process. I loved the writing, the reading, and sharing. Whether the haiku was "good" or not didn't matter. It was the same with my life. Whether I was treated as well as I wanted to be, or whether I was ignored, didn't matter as much as it had before, as I began to express what I wanted to say in essays, tanka, and haiku. My career, my marriage, my home became not things to "work on," but rather things to be with every day; observing how the day passed was enough in itself. As my writing horizons opened, my actual living horizons seemed to grow closer, and as they did, my life became more satisfactory. I wasn't looking out there for everything, I was looking right here on our half-acre lot.

As I became more observant, my heart started to open to the glories and terrors of nature, and the same of mankind. I no longer protected myself so much by hiding behind ambition and sales.

I didn't get into the Shinto feeling that some islanders have that everything has a spirit attached to it; "God in the raindrops" kind of thing. That's not my style. But I did become much more aware of the plants and animals in our vicinity and by extension, gave more time to the people who came within my range of attention too. I began to feel that people were not just to be judged by how useful they were to me — as I had been doing with our publishing business — but I started to feel out how useful people were to themselves. I suppose it was in this way that I began to encourage others to become creative.

I did become more intimately connected with the trees that we passed on the way to the beach: the two arbutus trees that nearly meet as they lean towards each other from either side of the road (I called them "the lovers") and the tree that had been downed in a recent storm so that it fell into the branches

of a nearby tree, which stood stolidly supporting it. In this way nature became an important part of life for me, as it fed both me and my haiku writing.

I began to find that taking a ginko every day allowed me to see my other concerns in somewhat better perspective. Particularly if Eli, my husband, and I had become overanxious about some problem, one or the other of us would just call out "Let's go!" and we'd drop the matter and wander down to the park. It was almost as though the walk fell into three phases to match the three lines of the haiku — the anxiety, the activity of the body, the relaxed focusing of the mind away from all those worries. The movement of our legs as we walked down through the trees formed the middle line of the haiku, pivoting me from one state of mind to another. In this way, haiku-walking became a tool to get me centered in myself again, with all my problems back in their proper places and proportions. Taking a ginko is a great way to transform depressive moments.

Two parts make one haiku. There must be a linkage present though; otherwise the poet is just making a list of what they have sensed. I started to realize how good I was at linking images and how that skill was really at the base of my poetry. I was beginning to see connections between supposedly unconnectable images, and that is what creativity is all about, I feel: the linking of two ideas that have possibly never been linked before.

Sometimes on these daily ginko I would catch only one line for a haiku. I wouldn't force the other two, but often, while sitting on the bench at the top of the park, those lines would appear as if the first line had just thrown out a hook and caught them up. I've never worked for a haiku, even when I've been asked for one on demand. Haiku come, or they don't come; you don't boss them around. Writing haiku taught me to relax and not bully life to go the way I wanted it to go.

Many haiku writers, on returning from a ginko, revise the

haiku they have written. I rarely do. If I do, it seems to lose the intensity of the first sense impressions. How can I be telling of the "now" when I am doing it later and have had time to reflect? While it's true that haiku are always written about a moment that has just passed, haiku-writing, I feel, isn't about reflecting. When I did occasionally revise, I felt I was concerned about the outcome, rather than just staying with the experience. If one realizes the moment is unique and never again to be experienced, why try to "improve" it by reflection later?

HAIKU AND
WABI—SABI

While modern Japan is as vulgar as modern North America, and even traditional Japan had its areas of grossness, two complex terms personify the best in Japanese aesthetics and Japanese poetry for me. They are the terms wabi and sabi. Their meanings have been modified with their history, but we could roughly say that wabi is concerned with the simple, with things of quiet refinement, the internal life. Sabi tends to be more concerned with outward aesthetic values such as elegant simplicity, the patina of aging, the irregularity of handcrafted things, the unpretentious, and the ambiguous. Both are concerned with imperfection, impermanence, and incompleteness.

When one is living life simply and directly, the ordinary becomes extraordinary just as the ordinary that is described in haiku becomes the wonder and amazement at life as it is, without asking "Why?" all the while. Haiku was never the poetry of the courts, but rather of the common man and woman. Haiku don't use obscure, multi-syllable, or academic words. We should take off all those distracting rings when we are pointing to the moon for people to look at. Just as haiku contain no unessential words, so is my life beginning to be stripped of the superfluous, the unnecessary, the unessential; it is becoming a wabi-sabi kind of life.

Somehow the marks of time of sabi things show how ephemeral everything is, how wear and tear has its own beauty. As it is with objects around us, so it is as we, ourselves, age. It is hoped our authentic self emerges as life shaves away our façade.

As I settled into myself and accepted myself, flaws and all, I started to accept the signs of wear and tear around me and not get anxious that everything didn't look sparkling and new. Old wooden cooking spoons that have helped make so many meals and furniture scratched and its varnish worn down from years of use all became sabi to me.

Haiku introduce a paradox: seeing directly but merely hinting at the seeing; finished but in some ways not finished; clear, yet ambiguous; nothing for sure. This gives them a certain melancholy that is perhaps the essence of wabi-sabi.

Even though I have a long and close marriage, the loneliness that sharply happens from time to time within any relationship accentuates the wabi-ness of life. The moments when I am awed by the immensity of the universe give me a humbleness; the same humbleness that penetrates so many haiku.

Footprints, shadows, things seen through the mist are all common elements in haiku-writing, and all introduce that wabi-sabi element that gives simplicity great value.

As I began to see the everyday in a new light (the beauty of garbage cans covered in snow), I also began to see that dark and light were inevitably to be found together, and that my despair should always be tinged with hope. Edward Weiss translates wabi-sabi as "sweet sadness," and I have come to view all my current writing as bittersweet, the wit tinged with tears, the mournful elevated by the absurdity of it all.

from wash basin
to wash basin, all is
nonsense

—Issa

Small things are examples of wabi-sabi and have come to be the essence of my life: thankfulness for hot water every day, for clean clothes to put on, for my husband's constant companionship. Fame and fortune cannot compare with these small moments of joy, moments that I have learned to appreciate more and more as my haiku writing progressed.

Natural, uncontrived . . . that's the essence of wabi-sabi and of haiku, and that is how my life should flow; no inner dialogues

about how I will say this or shouldn't have said that. Patience and awareness, the essence of haiku, are also implied in the qualities of wabi-sabi. It is the process that is to be appreciated, the patina that comes with aging. And, as I observe my own body scars, my liver spots, my aching joints, and weakening muscles, it seems as if my body has become a thing of sabi and my spirit a thing of wabi. My outwardly modest style of living gives me riches enough.

HEALING THE EARTH*

With the urgency of physical problems such as pollution and global warming, it seems odd to be urging people to write poetry, particularly those concentrated poems called haiku. In haiku you will find no despairing comments on the state of the planet. No "it's so bad!" or "it's so terrible!" Nor will you find overt comments on the awesome wonder of it all. What you will find is just what someone has sensed intensely at one moment in time.

You walk along and suddenly the smell of hyacinth will overwhelm you, the prickle of nettles on your legs will cause you to pause, the song of robins claiming their territory will assail you, the taste of the first spring greens from the garden will startle your palette, the vision of a blue jay tottering on a yellow sunflower will stop you on the path. At these moments,

---

*I wrote this piece for *Green Teacher* magazine, and since it shows how I was becoming more earth-conscious through my writing of haiku, I choose to include it here. It repeats some ideas already expressed, but that is to be expected.

all your senses are alert, you step out of the "everyday you," and find yourself in a strange new space. At these moments the haiku is born. You have to let your reader see, touch, smell, taste, and hear what you are sensing. The feelings within you at the time of writing will, you hope, rise in the reader as they read the haiku. It all depends on the degree of clarity with which you express yourself.

Haiku will not say how you have been overwhelmed, pushed out of your usual way of looking at things, given a fresh position from which to view the world; your haiku will merely state what you are seeing, touching, smelling, tasting, or hearing. But within those few chosen words, the moment you trap in three lines will have the ability to expand the scene you have written about until it involves the whole human condition, even the whole cosmos; that is, haiku-writing entraps you in the plant condition, the soil condition, and the weather condition. You and your environment become intensely linked when you write haiku. This identification with your surroundings can only lead to a deeper appreciation of how all life and non-life is interwoven on Planet Earth. As Clark Strand intimated, "[haiku is] the one form of poetry that makes nature a spiritual path."

But how can you write haiku when they need special moments for them to arise? Well it's true; you can't write haiku . . . haiku write you. But you can practice by not just learning the techniques of haiku-writing, but by observing things closely, becoming aware of your surroundings, and learning to choose words carefully to describe what you are sensing. Haiku demand you are totally "here now," and when you are, you receive the bonus of being everywhere at all times.

This all sounds a little remote from composting and caring for the land around you, but as to why you should try writing haiku at what seems like a crisis time for the earth, Bashō said: "You can learn about the pine only from the pine, and about the bamboo only from the bamboo . . ." I think this means that you have to identify, become one with what you are exploring, and then get the images down in writing. And I quote Bashō again, "In writing do not let a hair's breadth separate you from the subject." By identifying with a slice of time, a position in the world, you are opening yourself to the interconnectedness of all things. As Clark Strand says, "The Way of Haiku is to come 'unwrapped' and thereby notice what lies outside of the self. Without unwrapping ourselves, it is not possible to follow nature; it is not even possible to notice nature, much less to look carefully and with heart." And that is an important thing to be able to do these days, when we have to make so many wholesome decisions for ourselves, for mankind, and for the planet we live on. As Patricia Donegan states, writing haiku is "a deep way to practice deep ecology."

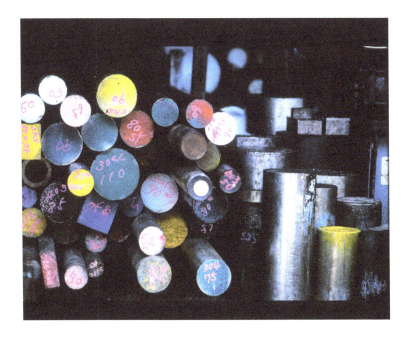

LOOSENING WITH LAUGHTER

I have always used laughter to loosen my audiences, to make a point instead of banging folks over the head. The healing power of laughter is so well known that it's almost a cliché to mention it. Haiku, which is ostensibly about the seasons, has its witty form pointing out our follies. It is called senryu. In senryu, we find the same condensed images that we do in haiku, but here the images are about the human condition, pointing out the ridiculousness and wonder of it all, including, of course, the ridiculousness and the wonder of me. Reading and writing senryu keeps me very humble and human; enabling me to laugh at, and so accept, my many faults.

Again in senryu, as in haiku, the images are simple and everyday, things that anyone could notice if they were aware; images that tell us that this reality is nonsense, that we can't explain it, so why waste energy trying? We are limited by our three dimensions and our five senses and none of us have the slightest idea what reality really is; we are all blind men describing parts of the elephant when we think we are telling about the whole animal.

Haijin often dispute whether a haiku is just that, or whether it is a senryu. I have actually never been at a haiku gathering where all those present agreed whether a certain three-liner was one or the other. So, before each of the following senryu, I should preface, "In my opinion."

For a very broad brush stroke, however, I would say that haiku concentrate on the seasons, and senryu focus on human nature, with, as Michael Dylan Welch adds, "a dash of humorous irony."

• • •

the laugh's on me:
this year's man
is last year's man

— Ching-An

We drag our old selves with us, no matter what new place, or as in this case, time (a new year) we go to. In many ways, I prefer senryu to haiku for making me feel at home in myself, because the foolishness of mankind that they portray makes my facial muscles relax — and sometimes my belly ones too — and restores every small trial I may have had to face to its correct proportions. Many senryu point out the illusory quality of this foolishness we call "life." At moments when the senryu strikes target, we can only let out a Zen laugh at this realization.

• • •

New Year's morning
the familiar smell
of burnt toast

— Carole MacRury

This one has a feel similar to the last senryu: a small domestic moment that makes one wonder whether anything will ever change. Our New Year's resolutions burnt to a crisp so soon, with the bread in the toaster. Senryu catch the sensing moment as do haiku; here "smell" sets the reader off on a thought trail.

. . .

morning paper
the dog brings me the news
already chewed

—Carole MacRury

Almost a political statement in noting this small moment — haven't the journalists and editors chewed up the news, slanted it, long before the dog got hold of the paper? Such senryu taught me to notice and give significance to so many small incidents in my day that I had formerly let fly past not caring.

. . .

baby boomers
our chin hairs
still... blowin' in the wind

—Terry Ann Carter

By alluding to a phrase from a popular song from younger days, Terry Ann defines the baby boomer generation so nicely here. Making allusions to others' poetry is a very traditional thing to do in Japanese haiku and senryu.

• • •

at my age
slowly
a snow angel

—Alice Frampton

Here is a minimal haiku that tells so much. This condensing
of ideas and feelings into simple images is so characteristic of
haiku and senryu writing. It is a discipline for verbal people
like me.

• • •

visiting mother —
again she finds
my first grey hair

—Michael Dylan Welch

The use of the word "again" seems purposeful, as if to say
that his mother can't remember that she repeats this action
at each visit from her son. The parental concern that one's
children don't age rapidly, don't show any sign of decay; and
should seem improved in some way at each visit are built into
mothers' genes.

• • •

one shopping day before Christmas . . .
a squirrel runs
from tree to tree

—Michael Dylan Welch

Two not very similar images and yet how they reflect each other as the squirrel runs wildly around storing for the winter and the Christmas shopper equally runs wild. This is a fine example of two juxtaposed images that reinforce each other.

• • •

Christmas concert —
in unison
the whole chorus inhales

— Michael Dylan Welch

That's how haiku/senryu get written; you note a small moment as somehow interesting. Only later do you see how profound that moment was as, in this case, it speaks of community and what can be done when a group of people are all of one voice. "In unison" implies the choir is all in tune, but then comes the nice turning that they are more than just in tune, they are breathing as one animated being.

• • •

aging rock star —
a hearing aid
in each ear

— Michael Dylan Welch

"Aging" and "hearing aid" go together and present no great depth. That the aging person is a rock star brings up the question of cause and effect. The singer has paid for his raucous stardom down the line. Perhaps it was worthwhile.

. . .

suckling the baby
in bed, she shakes her head
at her husband

— anonymous, Japanese

This reminds me of a cartoon I saw once of a couple in bed. The woman is saying "No, I don't have a headache; I have three kids and a full-time job." What else needs saying? Haiku and senryu always hit their target but never need to spell anything out.

. . .

no nagging on the day
her husband has a winner —
now there's a woman

— anonymous, Japanese

This is a terrible picture of a marriage and the endless demands couples can make of each other. Yet doesn't it strike home somehow? Don't we all reward good behavior that we approve of or that benefits us? Where's unconditional love? A fiction if ever I heard of one. Senryu taught me not to laugh at, but to laugh with, knowing I share so many human failings.

Senryu are in many ways my favorite form of haiku. Humor has always been my way of breaking up the twists and knots I get myself into so often. It's so great to have a poetry form that encourages one to open one's mouth wide and roar with laughter.

HAIGA — FREEING
THE ARTIST*

"Babble and doodle are two of the most primitive and universal human activities." So said Leon Zolbrod (1930 – 1991), long-time professor in the department of Asian studies at the University of British Columbia. He was speaking specifically of the words of haiku and the strokes of haiga — haiku being a traditional Japanese form of poetry and haiga being the paintings that sometimes accompany haiku. Since they come from the same brush, so to speak, they quite naturally developed together.

---

*My writing of haiku drew me into the world of haiga (haiku + image). Images are strong elements in haiku. By adding a painting or photograph to the haiku, as is done in haiga, the effect is even more pronounced. Haiku + image allowed me the joy of being able to join my love of art with my world of words, in this way enriching both. This is an essay I wrote for *Still Point Arts Quarterly* on the subject; again, some repetition is to be expected. As you'll see, the many characteristics of haiku are also reflected in the image chosen to accompany the haiku.

Traditional haiga — mainly from the seventeenth through the nineteenth centuries in Japan — is a composite form of art, consisting of haiku, calligraphy, and brush painting. These activities are paradoxical in that they must be infused completely and entirely with the concentration and vitality of the poet and the painter. Yet, somehow, the poet and the painter disappear, and one is left with only a few words and a faint picture. There is no evidence of the creator. It is as if in the concentrated moment the words wrote themselves and the painting emerged subtly from the void.

The essence of haiku and haiga is spontaneity . . . immediacy. Haiku and haiga are recording the senses: the sense of brushing past a bush of lavender from which the smell releases; the sense of tasting the first plum of the year; the sense of stroking a new baby's skin; the sense of hearing a temple bell in the distance; the sense of glimpsing a traveler on a road winding far off into the hills. Only impressions are called for. Words are in the present tense because it is the here and now being recorded. Bashō, the great haiku poet, said, "Haiku should be written as swiftly as a woodcutter fells a tree or a swordsman leaps at a dangerous enemy." Haiga, too, merely records the scene.

Such speed does not come without practice. Although anyone can produce a haiku or a haiga once if skillfully guided, it takes years of trying and failing to become accomplished. The technique must become so embedded that it doesn't show.

Besides technique, something else is required for a successful haiku or haiga and that is a state of innocence and clear seeing. Such a state results in there being no separation between the poet, the artist, and the work. No separation allows one to show how this is like this, rather than how this is like that. There is no room for didactic statements, moral judgments, social comment, or cleverness. There is nothing other than a recording of a sensing moment.

Haiku and haiga exemplify the quality of wabi-sabi — sparseness, roughness, loneliness, brevity, simplicity. No overflowing of words or brush strokes. Merely a hint, and yet that hint needs nothing added or taken away in order for the reader or viewer to be able to catch the original emotion that triggered the work. And from this state, for the reader and viewer are also part of the creative act, the overtones of the words and painting ring out to the ends of the universe.

The open-endedness of the poem and picture is paradoxically what helps capture the moment. The past is implied and the next action hinted at, yet the words and painting only tell of the present. No wonder Zen monks were practitioners of these arts. The many mysteries of the universe are hinted at when a petal falling from a magnolia blossom is spoken of and illustrated in direct simplicity.

Haiku and haiga are not neat things, not clever, polished and sophisticated. The image is roughly caught at whether by words or paint. An eye is a slit, a nose a small curve, a mouth goes up, or down to vaguely suggest joy, or sadness . . . and all this without effort. You can't try to paint a haiga using your intellect or when you are overwhelmed by emotions. In fact you can't "try" at all. Either the intensity that drives the brush is there, or it is not.

• • •

Traditional Japanese haiga were brushed beside the haiku, which often was written in one downward line. Buson's illustrations for Bashō's book *Narrow Road to the Deep North* are the best known haiga in the classical style. This haiga by Buson is a scene of Bashō embarking on a journey. No mention of journey in the haiku and yet it matches exactly the mood of sadness at Bashō's departure. Buson's haiku reads:

loath to let spring go
birds cry and even fishes'
eyes are wet

—(translated by Sonja Arntzen)

By the way, Bashō includes the word "fish" in the haiku because his journey to the deep north started at Senju, where there was a major fish market, so he would be starting his journey walking past the stalls of fresh fish, their eyes still glistening.

• • •

This painting by Buson illustrates his haiku about rocks. The rocks are roughly sketched and still their state of confusion or "scatteredness" is evident:

willow leaves are gone
the fresh brook has now run dry
rocks scattered here and there
                    —Buson (translated
                    by Sonja Arntzen)

• • •

This painting and haiku, again by Buson, is of a celebrant at a cherry blossom festival. Buson doesn't even bother to show cherry blossoms, just the empty sake gourd and the drunken reveler dancing. Anyone who has been to a cherry blossom festival would observe that the tradition of reveling continues even today.

> *yes, you will meet him —*
> *Matabei at Omuro*
> *cherry blossom time*
> — Buson (translated by Sonja Arntzen)

• • •

As with Buson's rocks, some haiga directly reflect on the subject of the haiku. Watanabe Kazan's sketch of morning glories is actually described in the haiku, explaining the essence of haiga painting in the lines "the clumsier you draw them, the more pathos they have." The Japanese word translated as "pathos" is a word that incorporates deep meaning and a certain nostalgic sadness: the fragility of the object adds to its beauty, for all must pass.

> *with morning glories*
> *the clumsier you draw them*
> *the more pathos they have*
> — Basho (translated by Sonja Arntzen)

. . .

Today, outside Japan, many haiga are done with digital photographs. A far cry, you might say, from spontaneity, as the photographer manipulates the image in an endless number of ways to his or her choosing. And yet the best photo-haiga equal in power anything Buson might have painted. Here is a photo-manipulated haiga by haiku and tanka writer, Carole MacRury:

empty bus stop —
one old crow looks
at another

The two small glimpses of white within the feathers somehow make the black much darker. No image of the other crow here, nor of the bus-stop, and yet somehow the simple

image includes them both. And not only does it leave room for them both, it also gives rise in the viewer to the idea that our journey in life is merely the waiting at a series of bus-stops, our fixed home as temporary as a stop at a caravanserai, and that as we grow old and our feathers droop this ephemeralness of life becomes clearer and clearer to us. Good haiga can produce such ideas and the usual accompanying sigh that goes with them.

• • •

Here is another haiga from MacRury. In this piece the illustration has seemingly nothing to do with the haiku and yet the fallen skin of the onion marks the passing of all things,

leaf fall. . .
how easily I slip
between seasons

and the sharp shadow implies that this reality may not be all it seems to be. The idea of Plato's cave with its shadows merely reflecting reality arises, perhaps. Certainly the idea of multi-universes we might be able to "slip between" allows for endless questions.

*leaf fall . . .
how easily I slip
between seasons*

• • •

Next is a haiga from Jim Swift who has developed photo-haiga to a fine art. This is an example of an abstract haiga which resonates so well with the accompanying haiku. There is a feeling of the coming and going at the airport, of the excitement of new adventures. And yet here too is a feeling of cycles, of the possibility that our lives are not as linear as they might seem. The closed shape on the left is reminiscent of the Japanese enso, the circle that is painted roughly by Zen master calligraphers, enclosing the void and yet symbolic of the moment. The two parts traditional in haiku and shown by the dash are repeated in the two almost separate shapes Jim has captured.

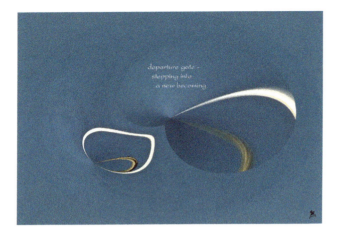

departure gate —
stepping into
a new becoming

Inspired to create your own haiga? Use a "thrifty" brush, go for the kokoro, the heart of the image being recorded. Try too hard and you miss the mark. Become the object and you can't go wrong.

LETTING IT ALL OUT
— TANKA

The Uses of Tanka

In Heian times,
tanka were sweet confirmations
between courtier lovers
of deeds done and to be done.
And also of court rapists,
for dark chambers and
many-layers of kimono
hid identities, so seducers
were never quite sure that
they had entered the right woman.
Even in such cases of mistake,
the next morning the maiden
would receive a token tanka
speaking of her long hair perhaps,
and other matters, and it would be
attached to the prescribed branch

from say a flowering cherry.
She, in return, whether mad with anger,
sulking, or perhaps with a small smile,
would be obliged to also write a tanka
in response, commenting on the situation,
and send it along with maybe
a late blooming plum blossom.
A few years later both women,
whether seduced, or once loved,
might be found writing more acerbic tanka
complaining of neglect, or at least
that the dwelling he had provided
for them was not up to par.
Tanka-writing would also be called for
when noblemen, at time of banishment,
(maybe for a political misstep, or
for the seduction of the Emperor's favorite)
thought sadly of the capital
they would be leaving for say
the beaches of Suma (always a good place
for writing mournful tanka of exile).
These days, I write tanka
when my haiku get uppity
with the conceit that they have
nailed the moment to the page.
I slap them with two extra lines,
reminding them that all things pass,
particularly the "here and now"
and even if things don't pass
as quickly as we would like,
it's all illusory anyway.
Yes, tanka are useful for times
such as these.

Well, this poem pretty well lets you know the uses of tanka, those five-line, free-verse poems written traditionally as 5,7,5,7,7 sound syllables* that have been written continually for over 1,200 years — haiku a mere 600. The five lines move from image to image, idea to idea, feeling to feeling, yet they flow seamlessly together to present a strong statement of humankind's place in the universe, even though the poem may be intensely personal. That is tanka's greatest attraction for me, the ability to combine my personal take on the world with a more detached view of the way the world runs.

One source of tanka, originally called waka, was the five-line envoi added to the choka (long poem). The envoi was often a kind of summary of what had gone before or a philosophical statement reflecting the theme of the choka.

Michael Dylan Welch points out that "tanka are not stretched haiku." Tanka, unlike haiku, introduce ideas and feelings directly.

Having established myself firmly in my body by writing haiku — the poetry of nouns — it was time to expand a little by exploring my thoughts and feelings through the writing of tanka — the poetry of verbs: loving, hating, yearning. No, it is not good to let all your feelings spill out after years of writing haiku, which don't allow them to be expressed overtly. But by the time I moved from writing haiku to writing tanka, all my feelings and ideas stowed inside haiku were ready to fall out onto the page, and I just let them. Expressing them as a commentary on a sense observation, as is often done in tanka, is a good way to stand back a little and see what is going on. Oddly enough the feelings that I avoided writing directly about when I was writing haiku seemed to have been

---

*When writing tanka in English usually somewhere between about twelve and thirty-one syllables are used.

transformed into deep and sincere feelings by the time tanka entered my life.

Tanka allowed me to express my unspoken shadow feelings. Once I started to get in touch with deep feelings that seemed familiar — yet at the same time old and distant — I needed to learn to view them in a non-attached way so I didn't cling to them, whether they were of joy, sadness, or anger. By expressing them in tanka, I was able to explore them dispassionately and hopefully realize how insubstantial they were. My feelings became more like comments as they removed themselves a few spaces from me in my practice of tanka writing.

The kick that often occurs in the last line, at least in tanka written in English, shot me out of any narcissism I might have had into sharing the human condition, mine being no different. Tanka allowed the narcissistic "I" to be removed to a distance, by shifting my personal drama's boundaries so they opened to involve all human beings' dramas. This happened because tanka writing, by exploring my thoughts and feelings, allowed me to view the world from a different perspective, a more tolerant perspective, as I came to realize my sufferings or pleasures are no different from anyone else's. The subjective states I expressed in tanka became just as valid to me as the objective words I chose to write in haiku. I began to balance my senses' registration with my emotional reactions and my ideas.

As I shifted from experiencing emotions to exploring them, the emotions started to seem absurd, excessive, or, at least relative. Tanka, by recording my many moods and fluctuating ideas, gave me the realization of my own insubstantiality.

By discussing some of my favorite tanka next, I can, perhaps, show you a little more clearly what tanka are and how they opened my being to the full range of human feelings and allowed me to express the modest amount of wisdom my years had granted me.

• • •

remember when
we picked green plums
young and impatient
we never waited
for the ripening

—Carole MacRury

Here is a tanka of nostalgia about the energy of youth, a time when one desired to experience everything and everything quickly, for there was so much to experience. The image of unripe plums on the trees reflects the unformed personality. The more fully developed being waits patiently for everything to come in its right season. An impatient person myself, I really absorbed the message of this tanka. There are pivot lines in tanka. See how the line "young and impatient" could complete the first two lines, or, alternatively, start the last two lines. Either way it tumbles you from the image of two young people picking fruit to stressing the impatience of youth.

• • •

spring yard work —
together we turn the earth
turn the worms . . .
the roots of our marriage
both forgiving and deep

—Carole MacRury

This is a tanka in which a domestically romantic image of a couple doing yard work together is a metaphor for all the mess that can be dug up in any long marriage, but that needs turning over, forgiving and forgetting. The expression "can of worms" comes to mind. This tanka is a deep statement on marriage, and all in five lines. In medieval Japan, tanka — called waka at that time — were the poems of relationships as lovers, marriage-partners, and close friends used them for their correspondence, in which they often told of their deep feelings for each other. Writing tanka, I was able to tell my husband how much he meant to me in a rich and meaningful way.

• • •

spring magnolia
so short this time of deep
pink blooming . . .
yet we pick to own
what we'll soon discard

— Carole MacRury

We spend our time acquiring things, perhaps because of their beauty or because everyone else has them, but then when they fade or we get bored, we quickly let them go. This reflects not just on the way we acquire material goods but on our relationships to them also. See how the personal image of the magnolia flower spills over into a philosophical statement about the way things are. I love the economy of tanka.

• • •

"mum, don't you
recognize my voice
any more" —
I blame the connection
but the truth is worst

— Amelia Fielden

This recording of a poignant moment says so much about Alzheimer's and the terrible effect it has on a family. Almost in a flash a person has gone from being fleshed out to being a ghost. The use of the word "connection" is important, since it not only implies the phone's connection is faulty but also a break in the human linkage.

. . .

seniors' outing —
becoming aware that
I've entered
the time zone where death parts
more often than divorce

—Amelia Fielden

This is such a clever way of defining aging. This tanka speaks so much to my own generation. As I age, tanka are such an easy way for me to express my fears for my future and my acceptance of the inevitable. Writing the fears down on paper in such a condensed form as tanka offers, shows me clearly where I am and what is yet undone and needing to be dealt with. Amelia uses the dash to allow that very necessary pause for our anticipation to build.

. . .

I miss you in this evening rain
and knowing that I have no idea
if you miss me too
makes me miss you
even more

—Michael Dylan Welch

This lovely tanka deeply illustrates the uncertainty that is in all relationships. Such tanka encourage me to not take my husband for granted, because although we have been together over forty years, often I seem to know so little about him.

• • •

how do ducks
stay afloat
on the water
when here on land
I feel myself drowning?

— Fujiwara no Shinzei (translated by Sonja Arntzen)

This amazing tanka reinforces the idea of the insubstantiality of everything we think is solid. Not just literally — land, but figuratively — our solid lives that we think will always stay the same. It reminds me that when I really consider how our earth is spinning around in space, I get giddy with the true insecurity of my place in things. A simple image reflecting a complex truth is a common format for tanka.

• • •

life in this world
is it not like a reflection
in a mirror?
there yet not there
but neither not there

— Minamoto no Sanetomo (translated by Sonja Arntzen)

This is a totally Zen tanka. I'd always wanted to be a student of Zen, which I had thought would suit me well. But no, life offered me Tibetan Buddhism with all its bells and whistles, while I secretly yearned for a black robe and a small hut. While haiku reflect a Buddhist outlook, tanka have space for the more paradoxical Zen statements.

• • •

how I wish
my tanka of passion
did not erupt
solely from old memories —
last night's storm is over

— Amelia Fielden

Fielden is a great writer of nostalgic tanka. She yearns for the intensity of passion from younger days, knowing that passion, like a storm, passes. Tanka is such a suitable form for writing of past years, no wonder I moved towards it as a way of expressing what I needed to say about times long gone, and such writing encouraged me to eventually get around to finishing my book of memoirs.

• • •

the years pass
yearning to fly free
love holds me still —
yachts moored near the pier
move just a little

— Amelia Fielden

Here the image — the slight movement of anchored yachts — usually in the first part of the tanka, is in the latter part. In this tanka, the fact that the yachts can move, if only slightly, contrasts with the firm hold that her present love has on her. Metaphor and simile can run riot in tanka whereas they are rarely shown overtly in haiku, where there is no time to compare "this" to "that."

As I was immersing myself in tanka writing, I began to realize that I couldn't possibly appreciate Japanese tanka as much as Amelia Fielden and Sonja Arntzen do because they are both translators and so very sensitive to the nuances of Japanese poetry, both the allusions and the language play. I started to wonder what my role could be. I already understood that while I had written the odd fine haiku, I lacked a real depth of understanding of the form. I had been giving haiku workshops for some time though, and I could see that I had the enthusiasm and enough understanding to introduce people to haiku. I decided I could do the same with tanka.

I am a person who skims, a supposedly negative quality. But supposing this ability was just enough for me to grasp the essentials and open the world of tanka — that I so loved — to others? This insight gave me fresh purpose in life, for while I continued writing poetry and essays for my books, I was free to announce my limitations when it came to writing Japanese poetry, and yet still be able to claim my skill at being able to inspire and encourage others to write. Could one ask for more — a purpose and a matching ability?

· · ·

the two mating flies
on the deck feet up
I, the ruthless
slayer of generations
sip green tea

— George Swede

Life ... death ... we only have power over them to a certain extent, and that lies in the ability to handle small concerns. Is God — if there is such a being — so thoughtless of his/her actions also?

. . .

"too young
to really be in love"
now too old
to stay awake all night
where did the between go?

— Amelia Fielden

She is the master of nostalgia, didn't I tell you? Tanka are for remembering, and the practice of tanka writing stirred me to give workshops on tanka as well as on writing memoir. And as I mentioned, it encouraged me to write my own memoirs. So tanka provided a practical direction for both my writing and teaching energies.

. . .

hilly paths
I walk where
once I ran —
sometimes the past
must be enough

—Amelia Fielden

The simple slowing down from running to walking says so much about aging. The introduction of the word "hill" suggests the uphill struggle of youth and the downhill movement of our bodies declining. The pivot line, "once I ran," fits well here as it uses a past memory to encourage our acceptance of the signs of aging.

. . .

half a tanka
will probably suffice
to say
this blur on life's page
is ready for erasure

—Sanford Goldstein

This master tanka writer muses on his life as must we all. He barely gives it half a tanka, almost wiping it all out, as if his life has had very little imprint on the world. In reality, Sanford Goldstein writes tanka every day and has had an enormous influence on the tanka-writing world, not to mention the world of his profession as a teacher and translator. Is it false modesty, a moment of depression, or his own true estimation?

As an aside, my immersion in daily haiku or tanka writing

allowed me to see that the post-partum blues I often had at the end of writing each book, and sometimes even after the writing of each poem, could be viewed positively as an indication that it was a time to withdraw and hibernate. Depression is only pathological when you get locked into it.

· · ·

I dance by myself
to an old favorite
on the radio —
my shadow seems
older than I

—George Swede

I have always loved shadows, ever since as a child I did the finger-play of shadows on a wall. Shadows seem to me to hold a truth deeper than the reality they are projected from. The poet is dancing, maybe like his younger self. His shadow reminds him that the past is only a shred of the present.

· · ·

entering old age
I look less for truth
but find it more —
a mid-winter thaw reveals
pieces of sky

—George Swede

This is a fine tanka by a brilliant poet. One of the paradoxes of old age is when one stops asking questions of the universe; it is then, somehow, that everything falls into place. The metaphor of this paradox, by using the image of the parting of perhaps heavy snow clouds to show bits of the sky, is wonderfully chosen. Both George's and Amelia's tanka on aging helped me move slightly more gracefully into my old age.

• • •

writing a poem
of longing for her
I'm irritated
by the interruption
of her phone call

— George Swede

Ah, the gap between the ideal and reality! This very witty tanka offers a profound truth, and that is why tanka so appeal to me. They help me take my personal reality to a level that everyone can share: his abstract muse is obscured for a moment as his real-life muse calls on the phone.

. . .

department meeting :
while the mouths utter business
the eyes ripple with
someone sailing, someone fishing,
someone drowning

— George Swede

Yes, we carry on the everyday smiling and functioning while underneath, as Stevie Smith so aptly put it, "we're not waving, but drowning."

. . .

a sudden loud noise
all the pigeons of Venice
at once fill the sky
that is how it felt when your hand
accidentally touched mine

— Ruby Spriggs

This is an often quoted perfect tanka by a distinguished Canadian writer, unfortunately now dead. Reading this tanka inspired me to go searching for more of her writing and wishing I had known her. Tanka can lead you out like that, I've found, as you share your humanity as the reader with the poet's as the writer.

. . .

How utterly vain!
The great old men of China
arguing reason

before they can articulate
the origin of things
> — Motoori Norinaga (translated by Sam Hamill)

This tanka doesn't have a description of a sense image, but it does have a subject: wisdom, or rather assumed wisdom. Norinaga asks how one can be wise when we don't know the origins of anything: what kind of universe we live in; whether there are parallel universes; whether we possibly exist in more than one place at once; why there is something instead of nothing. In fact, he is advising what Buddhist texts recommend: to not fret about life after death and other things impossible to know. Better to be here now, that is difficult enough.

• • •

spring flowers
seem the brightest
along the prison wall —
my bus today
happily late
> — Michael Dylan Welch

A seeming disconnect between the two images: the prison wall and the bus stop. Yet the vision of the spring flowers cleverly joins the rest of the lines together and explains the poet's happiness at the bus's delay.

• • •

a toothpick
stuck in the cake
comes out clean...

wishing it were as easy
to know when I've said enough

— Susan Constable

A common domestic image, but who would connect it with keeping one's mouth shut? The test is for whether the cake has cooked sufficiently, or not; if only there were a similar test for when we've said enough. Susan is a brilliant tanka writer and knows how to expand simple everyday events so that they involve us all.

• • •

it's come to this
he and I only
by turning the page
in our Japanese calendar
learn it's Valentine's day

— Sonja Arntzen

This is such a wonderful tanka portraying love that has settled down. A slight yearning for earlier days is implied, yet still their common interests and respect keep the couple joined together. It is a warm, very deep comment on relationships. Tanka allowed me to explore my over-forty-year relationship with my husband and express many things about our relationship that I had never done before.

• • •

another day
of waking to the scent
of sea-wrack . . .

ready to face the ebbs,
the slacks and tidal surges

—Carole MacRury

Here Carole parallels the ebb and flow of the tides with the ups and downs of her life. Smell is the trigger sense here. I love tanka that start with the sense image of haiku and expand to philosophizing with interesting metaphors.

• • •

once a young girl
standing alone at a bus stop —
now a woman
wondering what might have been
if she'd said yes to a stranger

—Susan Constable

Tanka is the perfect poetic form for expressing regrets, those "might-have-beens," those dangerous corners where the road divides and we are forced to choose. Only too often our conditioning has already done the choosing for us. Tanka are for stripping your conditioning, your inhibiting parameters, and letting things be told clearly and openly without guile.

• • •

too soon
first leaves fall
from the maple
this fear of losing
what defines me

—Susan Constable

This wonderful tanka compares the falling of leaves to the falling of our own, and perhaps others' image of ourselves. Without role definition, without branding, who are we? Tanka is the perfect form for asking deep questions, such as these, of ourselves and of the universe, and expressing our fears such as the one in this fine tanka.

. . .

*neighborhood wi-fi
down again —
the trains that pass
no longer end
with a red caboose*

— Michael Dylan Welch

Here Michael muses on technological advancements that may truly be amazing and yet stagger along in their complexity. He compares them with the good old-fashioned, reliable, technically simple things we used to take for granted, such as a red caboose at the end of a string of carriages and rail-cars. As Jung said, "Reforms by advances, that is by new methods or gadgets are of course impressive at first, but in the long run they are dubious and in any case dearly paid for."* A hint here of nostalgia for times past, times that our memory has elaborated in desirability.

As I see it, from a psychological point of view, haiku keep you centered in the body senses, grounded in the earth, more and more aware of the details of life. The grounding and centering of haiku-writing stilled my emotions and allowed my true feelings to emerge when I came to writing tanka. Emoting is not feeling.

---

*Carl Jung, *Memories, Dreams, Reflections*. Random House, Inc., 1961.

By speaking of memories and future desires, tanka-writing reminds us that all is illusion and passing, yet perhaps agrees with haiku-writing in that all we really have is the moment.

OPENING TANKA — RESPONSE TANKA

As I mentioned previously, tanka were commonly used for communicating between people, so, after being introduced to tanka-writing by Sonja Arntzen, she and I decided to try a book in which we linked our tanka by responding to each other's words. This introduced the trust factor for me; that is, would I be able to trust myself to open deeply enough to another person's feelings and also trust that they wouldn't stomp all over mine in response. I took a chance.

The first book-length set of response (or as some people say, "responsive") tanka we did together, *Double Take*, was so much fun, we decided to follow it up with a second book, *Reflections*. What follows is an excerpt from *Double Take*. In the first pair of tanka, Sonja responds to mine, and in the second pair, I respond to a tanka of Sonja's.

the cherry in full flower
is worthy of admiration
yet I prefer
the fall's spiraling keys or
the first green aura after snows

— Naomi

minor keys
move the heart deeply —
a garden where the blossoms
have fallen, rain
heard in the night

— Sonja

a strange cold spring
scant rations of sun
clouds with no rain
a sense of barrenness,
yet the world greens steadily

— Sonja

at the breakfast table
after a disappointment
a red-headed woodpecker
lands on the mountain ash
and the world is righted

— Naomi

When we worked on *Reflections*, we decided to use the poetry technique of honkadori, and I started the book by explaining this poetry form:

"Besides the response tanka that Sonja and I wrote here, we also tried to vary the form by using such old techniques as honkadori — in which we took a line from a foundation classic poem and incorporated it into our responses. This was a popular way of writing tanka (waka) from 1200 –1350 CE. Here we used lines from Steven Carter's *Waiting for the Wind: Thirty-Six Poets of Japan's Late Medieval Age*. The lines we chose were 'the midnight traveler' (from the tanka by Tamekane), and the line 'the contending cries of birds' (from the tanka by the Emperor Fuishimi). I gave my tanka first, using the chosen line, then Sonja's response, and then we added the original poem from which we had selected a line to use. Of course, if you were using the honkadori technique when writing in English, you would allude to a well-known line, or phrase in our culture."

As Sonja commented, "It was an enjoyable process that we recommend to other English tanka poets as an active way to engage with classical Japanese poetry in translation."

following
a star not in the Heavens
he ploughs ahead
looking to neither side
"the midnight traveler"

— Naomi

moon orange in smog
one pool of light on the station floor
furtive shapes to the side
seeking shelter for the night
spook "the midnight traveler"

— Sonja

He passes the inn
where he was to spend the night —

drawn on by the moon.
Already on tomorrow's path
is the midnight traveler.

— Kyōgoku Tamekane

And the second honkadori:

spring morning...
I have to deal with
a confusion of feelings
the demands of the garden
and "the contending cries of birds"

— Naomi

light floods the plain
of ocean, seeps between eyelids
banishes sleep,
opens the ears to
"the contending cries of birds"

— Sonja

From the mountain shades,
I look beyond the bamboos
to where the sun falls;
and throughout the grove —
the contending cries of birds.

— Emperor Fushimi

A couple of years later I did a book of response tanka with the performance poet David Bateman. As David is an academic and citified and I am domestic and countrified, the contrast in our styles was rather noticeable and I not only had to trust David would understand what I had written from my rural base, but I had to try extra hard to penetrate his tanka as they were dense with metaphors and similes. We did this book differently from the way Sonja and I did ours, which had been a simple call and response. For *pause* — the book David and I did — I sent David a tanka, he responded and then, as if reconsidering things, he sent one responding to the one he had just sent, and then I did likewise. So it was as if we were adjusting our own response, a chance one doesn't get every day in life. David chose to stick to the Japanese 5, 7, 5, 7, 7 sound syllables, although I pointed out that they were not relevant to tanka writing in English since the Japanese sound syllable doesn't correspond to the English syllable. I think he liked the discipline. We went on to perform the book in public together, and it was a pleasant surprise, I think, for the audience to hear this unfamiliar form of verse written by two very different poets.

my day off —
I immediately put in a wash
prepare a soup
settle down to write, but . . .
it feels different

— Naomi

by myself at home
organizing lives I've known
evaporating open
radiance of sunlit panes
cathartic craze Sunday's purge

— David

Freud's divan disguised
pillows upon pillows lounge

reluctant comfort
the transplendent luxury
nooks and crannies, cluttered spoils

— David

the afternoon couch
the perfect place to hate
one's parents
dredge up the past and
blame it on someone

— Naomi

BEING IN COMMUNITY

After having opened myself to other people at a deep level by writing two books of response tanka with Sonja Arntzen and one with David Bateman, I decided to expand my cooperative writing by writing renku with a third person added. In renku, the poetry contributions alternate between three lines and two lines. The segues are not as obvious as in response tanka where often the same image and a few of the same words may go into the response. Here each section has rules controlling it that are set out before the poets begin. They may demand "two lines about the moon, but with no mention of love," or "three lines about autumn with no mention of moon."

I started my venture into teamwork by doing a thirty-six-section renku with just one other person, Vicki McCullough, a fine haiku and tanka writer. We called our effort "Nudged By the Wind." In renku, authorship is switched after the sixth, eighteenth, and thirtieth verses, where the same person responds to their own verse. In this section, Vicki took the 3-lines.

Side One:

fish scales sequin   *(summer)*
the porcelain sink —
the uninvited wasps

         —Vicki

ocean bioluminescence   *(summer)*
makes us angels as we dive

         —Naomi

down the road   *(summer)*
bluegrass jammers singin'
'bout God's golden shore

         —Vicki

an empty rocking chair   *(no season)*
nudged by the wind

         —Naomi

stopped atop a Ferris wheel   *(autumn, moon)*
she reaches
for the moon

         —Vicki

raccoons share our crop   *(autumn)*
of coronation grapes

         —Naomi

When you are doing cooperative writing, whether with two or more poets, you have to listen carefully, not just to the words they are using, but to their intent underneath. By writing response tanka and renku, I gradually opened my talents and shared them with others. It was difficult for me to be patient while I waited for the other writers to supply their lines and difficult for me to dig down far enough to understand the deep feelings behind the images they were offering so I could respond suitably. Writing response tanka and renku is a good practice for a marriage or any other cooperative venture.

Later I did a renku with the fine poets Sonja Arntzen and Kim Goldberg. Again the links were defined by the rules, but they may seem more like leaps to the reader. Here are the last three sections from one of our renku:

Kasen Geese at Sunrise

Begun August 1 and completed August 3, 2012, on Gabriola Island. Poets were Sonja Arntzen (Sabaki), Kim Goldberg, and Naomi Beth Wakan. Based on a template (with a few adaptations) taken from "Throughout the Town," the 1690 kasen sequence composed by Bashō, Kyorai, and Bonchō, translated by Earl Miner in Japanese Linked Verse (Princeton University Press, 1979), pages 300 – 315. Suggested topics are in brackets.

Side Two:

a blanket spread   *(spring)*
under the cherry blossoms
teens work their iPhones

—Naomi

from spit and spiderwebs   *(spring)*
a hummingbird building its nest

—Kim

Spring burgeons
just beyond the edge
of his sick bed

(spring)

—Sonja

passing the department store
she considers a little black dress

(winter, miscellaneous)

—Naomi

snowflakes dance
in the headlights, dusting trash
in the gutter

(winter, miscellaneous)

—Kim

he reaches for her hand
begging her to understand

(love)

—Sonja

different desserts
she leans over to give
him a taste

(love)

—Naomi

human memory of each flavor
uploaded to cloud storage

(miscellaneous)

—Kim

this hemisphere's
autumn moon serene as
the rocket ship lifts off

(autumn, moon)

—Sonja

things coming, things going,   *(autumn)*
the year turns towards its end

—Naomi

skeletons appear   *(autumn)*
in windows, small ghosts
mob front yards

—Kim

a bagpipe echoes down the street,   *(miscellaneous)*
down decades, down centuries

—Sonja

Side Three:

in search of gold   *(miscellaneous)*
how many have been overrun?
how many destroyed?

—Naomi

pouring the kettle over ants   *(miscellaneous)*
my karmic debt swells

—Kim

"they are already dead"   *(miscellaneous)*
the advice given to Krishna
on the battlefield

—Sonja

shelling peas at the table   *(miscellaneous)*
the afternoon sun slants in

—Naomi

grebes running   (miscellaneous)
atop the water pursuing
weightlessness

—Kim

reeds bend into the pond   (autumn)
a tracery of reflection

—Sonja

drummers silhouetted   (autumn, moon)
against the red moon
so near yet so far

—Naomi

blood pounding in his ears   (autumn)
the trail mapped in golden leaves

—Kim

I turn away   (miscellaneous)
pick up the fallen shawl
huddle in darkness

—Sonja

we have to dive into the past   (miscellaneous)
to retrieve our missing parts

—Naomi

new in town, no chance   (love)
of running into anyone
she's had sex with

—Kim

seals lie languorously   *(love)*
side by side on the rocks

—Sonja

Side Four:

vows   *(love)*
made by the body
never last

—Naomi

"Do firs feel the weight   *(love)*
of their limbs?" the crone asks

—Kim

smell of pitch   *(miscellaneous)*
on the palm
sticky comfort

—Sonja

spring thaw   *(spring)*
the sound of ice cracking

—Naomi

the first cherries   *(spring, blossoms)*
to blossom are always
in the mind

—Sonja

geese at sunrise — blinded   *(spring)*
until I close my eyes

—Kim

Renku is writing in community. When I became poet laureate of Nanaimo, I began to literally write for a community. Other poets feared losing their focus with such a position, but I knew that most poets have only one thing to say. I knew that I could declare my "truth" whether I was writing about the seasons or about Nanaimo Bars, since for me everything is bittersweet, that strange mix that denies me unalloyed joy, or, indeed, complete despair.

HAIBUN — THE JOURNEY

Haibun means haikai writing, and haikai means something not exactly vulgar, but definitely not courtly or dignified. A haibun often describes a scene or an episode from actual travels as notes in a travel diary, except that a haiku is embedded in it or added at the end. The haiku can exactly match the scene, or it can just reflect the mood. The haibun itself can be real or imaginary. The word "haibun" was first used in 1690 by Bashō, the haiku master. His best known haibun was "Narrow Road to the Interior." Other famous haiku writers who tried the haibun form were Buson, Issa, and Shiki. Today haibun written in English is becoming increasingly popular, and folks such as Michael Dylan Welch, Jim Kacian, Susan Constable, and David Cobb have written some wonderful ones.

Here's a touching haibun by Susan Constable that doesn't involve actual travel, unless it be travel into the past:

. . .

Turning Point

My mother-in-law stares out the window as I sort ninety-three years of her life into "keeps" and "giveaways." A few months ago, she was unwilling to get rid of anything. Today, on the brink of moving her to the seniors' home, deciding what's needed or of sentimental value is up to me. She no longer cares, shows no reaction as I pull our dead son's T-shirt from her rag bag . . . dust her furniture for the last time.

house sparrows
at the empty feeder
winter deepens

I picked up this form of poetry + prose as my essay writing started to dominate my writing output. I used not only haiku and tanka within my essays but also inserted free verse. The poetry seemed to sum up what I wanted to say more succinctly than my rambling writing, which never seemed to come to the point. I called this form of writing espoe (essay + poetry), and it has become my distinctive way of writing. Oddly enough the study of haibun probably helped me recall the essay form I used when I was in high school, a time when I rarely submitted a homework essay without it having a quotation at the beginning and at the end. Quotations are condensed wisdom, and so that tug from the past must have slanted me towards the use of poetry — also a condensed form of wisdom — within my espoe form.

And I, on my healing haiku/tanka/renku journey, what have I left to say? In a way it has only reinforced what I have known already:

The end of suffering is not achieved by moving to a state from which I am radiating unconditional love or reaching some imagined state of perfection. (Perfection equals paralysis in my book.) It is achieved through awareness. Mark Epstein said, "Awareness allows you to experience terror without fear and delight without attachment." Haiku, by guiding me into the clear description of things, removed my judgmental attitude towards many of the things I was writing about. Haiku are "naked" poems, reminding me of the small guileless child I once was.

By writing haiku I came to learn the power of the small and how, by noticing detail, one's experience can stretch way beyond the object.

Haiku restored interest in my day-to-day chores. I no longer sought novelty or yearned to be "where the action is." The action was on our half-acre. I wasn't lost, I was here.

I learned that the ability to attend to the moment-to-moment nature of mind allows the self to be experienced without the distortions of overly positive or overly negative judgments of things. It also allows the objects of my sensing to be viewed in a fresh and probably more accurate way. If I don't give bare attention, I get lost in a confusing world outside and a threatening world inside. Dispassionate interest is what I need. I shouldn't screen out unpleasant facts; I should just observe them without judgment. By viewing things in a dispassionate way, one becomes a more "open" person. When I'm not clinging or avoiding, I can just be "interested," my emotions transmuted to interest in the object I am describing.

Writing haiku, I learned to stretch my sensing muscles, so that over the years I became more aware of details, didn't skim so much, and dwelt more on objects instead of quickly dismissing them.

I learned that only when I am not always reacting can I become my true self. Writing haiku showed me the way, for it confined me to the parameters of purely speaking of the nouns of images. This discipline allowed me to be more focused and not so scattered.

I began to do something I had never done before, and that was to value all the therapy and all the meditation I had done in life. I began to see them not as some exotic distraction, but as steps on the way to clear seeing, the clear seeing that I needed for writing haiku. My work as a therapist had helped me to look outwards without flinching too much at humankind's inhumanity; perfect training for tanka writing, where I could comment without attachment on my own and others' follies. Until I had detached myself from my emotions, I couldn't make the changes I wanted to make happen. Meditation taught me how to focus, which was perfect for the attention to subtleties that haiku demands.

By writing tanka, which brought up feelings and allowed them to be expressed directly, I learned that if I haven't dealt with past traumas, greed, hatred, and delusion can fester around them, making me defensive and isolated. When you have had a trauma, the techniques you use to adapt to such an intolerable situation become repetitive and meaningless. To break the cycle, trauma can become a matter on which to meditate. My challenge was to re-experience the trauma fully and then slowly defuse it by repetition until it no longer had power over me. Tanka helped so much in this respect. Writing tanka circling around my traumas gradually allowed me to feel them fully. Replay didn't remove the traumas, but it did help loosen their power over me.

I learned that pursuing pleasures can only lead to dissatisfaction. Either I can't get what I think is pleasurable, or if I do get it, I find it is ephemeral. Either way it can only cause suffering. Again, the philosophical ideas that arose by writing tanka helped me grasp this.

I learned that sex, food, and comfort won't satisfy. It is only in moments of intense creativity that I am able to suspend my constant self-consciousness that all is not as it should be. I owe this awareness to all my forms of writing.

I find I listen to people and react to them very differently these days. Somehow I stand back and watch my reactions and, at the same time, identify with the speaker, which allows me an empathy I never had before. The objectivity of just observing comes with haiku writing as well as the ability to become at one with the object observed — living the other person from the inside, as it were.

Even though haiku, tanka and renku writing have taken me to a place where I can restore my balance fairly quickly,

I realize that some days will still be downers and a few moments rather hellish. Why would it be otherwise?

I learned that healing consists of moving myself from my personal predicaments to the predicaments that confront all human beings. This is not enough in itself, however, for while writing, I have to return, time and time again, from my state of absorption to reality, bringing the message that life is insubstantial and ever evolving. I live inside, and yet my focus on Japanese poetry forms has taken me more consciously outside than ever before. Watching my passing moods, so I can't quite pin down who is the "I" that is watching, oddly enough makes me feel more "real," more alive.

It would be very foolish to claim that writing in Japanese poetry forms can heal everything, or indeed anything, or that the reader could get benefits similar to what I achieved by following my path. I did not plan these last thirty years (at least not consciously), but I didn't resist what they offered. I didn't emerge as some enlightened being. I am still dull mentally; from time to time I just don't "get" things. I am still naïve and jump to conclusions when given the scantiest bit of evidence. I still get sad and often think mankind isn't worth the time of day. But most days, I am filled with the joy of writing poetry, whatever the source may be, and that filling keeps me fully alive and urgent to the day's demands. Where I am is acceptable and for that I am grateful.

· · ·

I am this bundle of what has been, and what has been accomplished.
— Carl Jung*

Drawing to a close on these reflections of my poetry journey, I clearly see a parallel with Jung's four cognitive functions: intuition, intellect, sensing, and feeling. Writing haiku accentuated the importance of using my senses with clarity. Tanka writing allowed me to explore my feelings and intellect. For the cooperative writing of response tanka and renku, I needed to have confidence in my intuition to feel out what my co-writers were trying to say so I could respond in an appropriate manner. I started to see how the body is, in its own strange way, a repository of a certain kind of knowledge, a certain kind of wisdom. I began to trust it as I have never done before.

It has been a long, slow trip, but it has helped balance my being and has given me the skills to keep it in balance. The side benefit has been the creation of maybe a few rather nice poems.

I have come to see that in creating poetry, I am creating myself. Just as haiku cut down to the essentials, so I am paring my own life down to its basics. It is the "unencumbered life" that Leonard Koren recommends that I am starting to enjoy. Can one ask for more?

---

*Carl Jung, *Memories, Dreams, Reflections*. Random House, Inc., 1961.

ACKNOWLEDGMENTS

My thanks to Michael Dylan Welch, Alice Frampton, Carol MacRury, Amelia Fielden, Vicki McCullough, Sanford Goldstein, Ruth Yarrow, Jim Swift, Sonja Arntzen, Kim Goldberg, DeVar Dahl, Winona Baker, David Bateman, and George Swede for allowing their writings to be included. Most tanka written by these poets can be found in issues of *Gusts,* an excellent magazine of tanka published by Kozue Uzawa.

Thanks to Sam Hamill for the use of his translation of Motoori Norinaga's tanka, found in his book *Only Companion;* to Steven Carter for his translation of *Waiting for the Wind: Thirty-Six Poets of Japan's Late Medieval Age;* and to Sonja Arntzen for all her translations.

A deep bow in respect to Christopher Herold, one of my teachers . . . although he may not be aware that he was.

ABOUT THE AUTHOR

NAOMI BETH WAKAN is a poet and personal essayist. She has produced over fifty books, her latest being *The Way of Tanka* (Shanti Arts, 2017). She is the Inaugural Poet Laureate of Nanaimo and the Inaugural Honorary Ambassador for the Federation of British Columbia Writers. She lives on Gabriola Island, British Columbia, Canada with her husband, the sculptor Elias Wakan.

— www.naomiwakan.com

CPSIA information can be obtained
at www.ICGtesting.com
Printed in the USA
BVHW02s2045160418
513503BV00022B/767/P

9 781947 067288